Pasha Stories:

A Fairly Faithful Account of a Dog and His Person

By Robin Arbiter

I0159320

Sunnycrest Press • Springfield, IL

For all the family dogs: Daisy, Lady Dear, Angus Og, Isabel Blue, Tom Bombadil, Bilbo Baggins, Clara Bow, Goldberry, Galadriel, Miss Bianca, Cherie, Bjorna Bunchberry, Theodore, Freya, Katya, and all who came after, including Hershey, Sybil, Hodge-Podge, Mr. Bear, and Melody, Flora-Dora, and Pasha. The gift of your love outlasts the span of your years.

Text Copyright © 2016 Robin Arbiter,
Illustrations Copyright © 2016 Jerry Barrett

Summary: This book is based on conversations occurring between Pasha and Robin Arbiter in the dog-human dialect of their home. Mistranslations are entirely the fault of the human. Drool marks are almost entirely the fault of the dog.

ISBN 978-0-9970670-1-9

Visit www.sunnycrestpress/Pasha
office@sunnycrestpress.com

Introduction

Pasha was still a puppy when he came to me. I was middle-aged. Now we are both middle-aged, and in all honesty, Pasha is wearing this better than I. In the near-ish future, while I am still middle-aged, Pasha will be old. Pasha doesn't agonize over this because he lives in a time called NOW. I don't agonize over this because caring for Pasha means I must also live in the NOW, which, in the company of a dog, is a place of happiness, forgiveness, and gratitude.

Me: Seriously, Pasha, is there any surface you respect?

Pasha: (Looks puzzled, doesn't move)

Me: You're sitting on the coffee table.

Pasha: Coffee what?

Me: Table.

Pasha: (Cocks head) Table whaaat?

Me: Never mind.

Me: What's wrong? Are you sad?

Pasha: (Stares mournfully out window)

Me: What is it? What do you need?

Pasha: (Sighs deeply)

Me: (Hugs dog)

Pasha: Do you- have any- beef?

Pasha: I have a funny feeling.

Me: OK, let me get the leash and get you outside.

Pasha: Nope, don't think so. Sorry.

Me: No, no, no... Oh, rats.

(A pause while both of us stare)

Pasha: I feel a little better.

Me: Um, is that- why is that green?

Pasha: The bunny gave me his breakfast.

Me: Why is the bunny shivering?

Pasha: I don't know. Let's play!

Neighbor: Hey, your window was open, and I saw your dog standing on the bunny's cage, trying to climb up the bookshelf.

Bunny: (Conveys with terror-rounded eyes that there was some kind of hairy eclipse of the sun)

Me: Pasha!? Did you canine-eclipse the bunny by sitting on his habitat?

Pasha: When you swept, you picked up MY FAVORITE TOY and left it on a shelf.

Me: You have 20 toys. Which is your favorite?

Pasha: The one I can't reach.

Me: Darn, I forgot my glasses.

Pasha: That's ok.

Me: Maybe we should go back.

Pasha: (Throws himself down and rolls)

Me: Did you find something stinky?

Pasha: I don't think you'll want to see this.

Me: What's dripping off your head?!

Pasha: Dead bird? Squashed worm? Baby birdy eggs? Garbage? Duck poop?

Me: C'mon. What is it?

Pasha: No, seriously: I'm asking you.

Me: Stay away from that!

Pasha: What is that alluring sound?!

Me: Seriously! It will sting you!

Pasha: (Pounces on the window sill)

Pasha: It will have to sting me from the inside.

Me: Let's clean out your hidey hole.

Me: Old towel?

Pasha: Cloak of Invisibility!

Me: Chewed-up chew toy?

Pasha: Artifact of 1000 aromas!

Me: $100 shoe?!

Pasha: Never-ending dessert? Which you could still wear, as I've only nibbled out from the buckles.

Me: (It rained today) Pasha got muddy.

Pasha: The frogs were hiding, but I could smell them.

Pasha: They smelled delicious!

Pasha: I had to dig around for them.

Me: You got mud everywhere.

Pasha: You're welcome! Now *you* smell delicious!

Me: I had a hard day.

Pasha: Me, too.

Me: I didn't have a moment to myself all afternoon.

Pasha: I was alone forever.

Me: I'm HOME!

Pasha: Yippee! Yay! Howdy! Joy! Whee!

Me: I smell something.

Pasha: Me, too! I was walking around in a circle in the kitchen, and the second time around, there was poop on the floor!

Me: Um...

Pasha: Weird, huh?

Me: Wow. Look at that sky.

(Thunder, lightning, streaming rain and water)

Pasha: Mommy.

Pasha: Mom!

Pasha: Mommeeee!

(Big snuggle)

Me: I'm not saying who, but one of us is very afraid of storms.

Me: Five minutes.

Pasha: OK.

Pasha: Now?

Me: Five more minutes?

Pasha: It's up to you. There could be consequences.

Me: I'm up!

Me: Kibble? Water? Toy? Out?

Pasha: (Barking)

Me: What?! Why? What?

Pasha: I HAVE SOMETHING TO SAY, AND IT IS REALLY IMPORTANT!

Me: Kibble? Water? Toy? Out?

Pasha: It's like talking to a child.

Me: You can sleep on the bed, just not in the middle.

Pasha: Yippee!

Me: Not in the middle.

Me: Not in the middle.

Me: Not in the-

Pasha: Please don't kick me.

Me: Some dogs come when they're called.

Pasha: Not me! When you call, it's my cue to run faster.

Me: You see where it gets you though.

Pasha: Mm... Not really.

Me: Do the words, 'tackled in the parking lot by our city councilman' resonate at all?*

Pasha: Oh, yes! Boy, he really came out of nowhere.

---

*Our city councilman, Dennis, does not regularly go around tackling dogs. But he does have a wide view of community service, and we are grateful. Well, I am grateful, and Pasha still likes Dennis.

Me: I'm home!

Pasha: Hi! Hi! Hi!

Me: How was your day?

Pasha: OK. Did you talk to the neighbors yet?

Me: Should I?

Pasha: Probably not.

Me: (Intercepted near car by Neighbor Beth while walking Pasha)

Neighbor Beth: Hey, the maintenance man accidentally let Pasha out today.

Me: Damages?

Neighbor Beth: Well, he did his usual circuit around the cul-de-sac looking for bones and squirrels. Everyone's door was open because of the good weather. So, Pasha entered three apartments in sixty seconds, piddling in two of them, frightening one couple when he showed up at their breakfast table, breaking Mrs. Sweet's necklace when she tried to stop him, and stealing the poodle's treats at Grandma Susie's, where the maintenance man finally caught up to him. He was carried home in shame. Everyone was watching.

Me: Tell me his exact route, so I'll know what apologies need to be made.

Pasha: They don't need to apologize: I had a great time!*

---

*Apologies and restitution followed: I left Pasha home while I made these.

Pasha: She ran my foot over with her wheelchair.

I yelped.

Then she yelped.

I licked her face to let her know we were OK,

But she just cried and cried and hugged me.

Our friend Tami had to help settle us down.

Me: Shhh. (Pasha is snoring)

Pasha: (Yelps. Comes flying out from under the sofa)

Me: Oh, you poor thing!

Pasha: Fart Monster! Fart Monster! It grabbed my butt and sprayed a horrible scent. Horrible!

Me: I don't understand why you don't understand farting after eight years.

Pasha: If you want to write about people farting...

Me: I don't.

Pasha: But if you did... Remember that time we were on the couch, and I had to get down because you-

Me: No, I don't remember.

Pasha: There's cheese in the kitchen.

Me: (Silence)

Pasha: You know I'm a cheese dog, right?

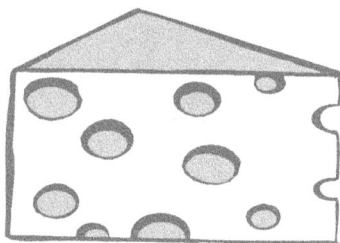

Me: I wrote a poem about you.

Pasha: Really?? Is it bacon-y? Beef-y?

Me: No, no: it's just words that describe you in Limerick form.

Pasha: So: nothing I can smell, chase or eat?

Me: No.

Pasha: Oh.

Me: Right. I'll go get you some kibble-snacks.

Pasha: And maybe some cheese?

Here is the Limerick about Pasha:

A Cocker Spaniel named Pasha
Grew tired of salmon and kasha.
"Why can't I just bite
A squirrel in flight
Or one that's a little bit squash-a?"

Things We Have Thought on Our Way Out the Door

Me: The joy of a happy dog is contagious.

Pasha: I look in the mirror, and all I see is god!
(Just kidding)

Pasha: Ohboyohboyohboyohboyohboyohboy!

Me: You know we're writing this book.

Pasha: Uh-huh.

Me: Should we call it Dog Tales? Oh- or what about Dog Tails? Is that too cutesy?

Pasha: I'm going to lick some part of myself and pretend you didn't just ask me about a pun involving spelling. A pun. Involving spelling.

Me: I think I need to call a friend.

Pasha: I think you need to give me a treat or two. One for being a good dog generally and another for this confusion here.

Me: I said I'd feed you as soon as I finished showering.

Pasha: I fed myself!

Me: Please don't tell me you've taught yourself a new trick.*

Pasha: No trick. Seriously, from now on, just put my food in that plastic can you're always yelling at, and I can get to it any time.

Pasha: Did you know there were chicken bones in there? They were down at the bottom, all wrapped up, like someone was trying to hide them. I ate them all and left the potato-y smoosh stuff for you.**

---

*Something I discourage since the great cookie grab of '08.
**This is why organic garbage is sometimes kept in the fridge now.

Me: It's 10:00 P.M., it's raining, and it's freezing. I can't take my wheelchair off the porch. You've got fifteen feet of leash. Please just walk yourself in the yard and do what you need to do.

Pasha: I don't want to get mud on my toes. I just don't. No, no, no.

Me: Really? You pooped inside, stepped in the mess, and left a paw-print trail throughout the house not six hours ago.

Pasha: Yaaasss… But you'd left me…

Pasha: Which makes it your fault.

Me: (Silence)

Pasha: I forgive you. Can I come in now?

Day 100: Still no peace between Pasha and the vacuum cleaner.

Day 99: Pasha, uncertain as to whether I understand his dismay at being left, ever, adds to his methods of communicating this.

Note to self: *buy more floor wash.*

Day 87: With leaves falling, Pasha, at window, sees more clearly the squirrels in the trees.

Note to self: *make another batch of glass cleaner.*

Day 70: During our walks, Pasha has eaten frog, cicada, earwigs, and randomly tossed chicken bones.

Note to self: *we are almost out of the seventy-dollars-per bag of dog food Pasha requires due to his intestinal sensitivity.*

Day 1: Left Pasha twice today. He is eight, has lived with me seven-and-a-half years, but is unconvinced I will return after leaving. Today's evidence? Dander bombs, cushion displacement, tumbleweed-sized hairballs, drool pool on the windowsill, paw prints on the coffee tables.

Note to self: *buy a vacuum.*

Me: What? What is that??

Pasha: (Foaming at the mouth, spits something onto wheelchair ramp)

Pasha: Nothing.

Me: Is that—a dead frog?

Pasha: Killjoy.

Me: (Picking up pamphlet) Where did this come from?

Pasha: Some people. They wanted to talk about going to Heaven.

Pasha: What's Heaven?

Me: A better world.

Pasha: There's a world with something better than belly rubs and squirrel hunts?

Me: (Kissing Pasha's nose) Probably not.

Pasha: If we're going, at least pack some treats. And a towel. And the Shoe Chew- that's my favorite. I'll carry it. And my water bottle. And my long leash.

Me: (Kissing Pasha's nose again) We're staying here.

Epilogue

Pasha: (Ambling along) So what was that Landofmilkandhoney they were talking about?

Me: Oh, well, in dog terms, a place with everything you could want-

Pasha: Like treats so yummy?

Pasha: Cheese and bunny?

Me: Yup.

Pasha: Hey, we have to stop here. See where that bigger dog keeps posting his message? I'm pretty sure I can lift my leg a little higher than that.

Me: OK, my little pumpkin-belly.

Pasha: You know my belly's not really made of pumpkin, right?

Me: Yup.

Pasha: Good, because that would be weird. Wow. Squirrels would want to eat me: that would be- oh, look, there's one now- that would be- and I let him go: who's a good dog now?

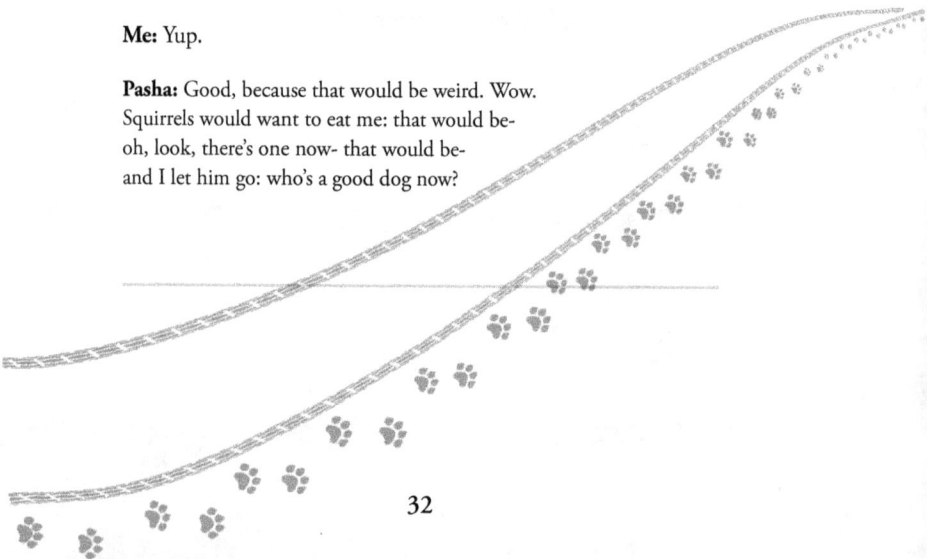

www.ingramcontent.com/pod-product-compliance
Lightning Source LLC
Chambersburg PA
CBHW060647030426
42337CB00018B/3486